Independent Social Work – A Risky Business?

Some Reflections from the Independents' Forum

Edited by
Gail C. Tucker
Anne Sambidge
and Helen Ogilvy

VENTURE PRESS

BASW website: http://www.basw.co.uk

Published by
VENTURE PRESS
16 Kent Street
Birmingham
B5 6RD

British Library Cataloguing-in-Publication Data
A catalogue record for this book is available from the British Library

ISBN   1 86178 073 7 (paperback)

Printed by:
Hobbs the Printers Ltd
Brunel Road
Totton
SO40 3WX

Printed in Great Britain

Contents

Foreword

It is thirty years since I qualified as a social worker and in that time there have been huge changes for social work. The political context and the organisational structures in which it works have radically changed. The division between commissioning and providing social care is firmly established. There has been a massive expansion in the range of private sector and voluntary sector providers as the statutory services focus more on commissioning and less on providing. In the public sector social workers now find themselves increasingly working alongside professionals in health, housing and education services.

People who use social care services are becoming increasingly involved in the way services are run and developed. The introduction of direct payments gives control to individuals over the services they require. People who use services are becoming social work practitioners, are involved in the education and training of social workers, in the governance of social care institutions, in research and in building up new provider organisations which they lead.

The social work profession has been strengthened. It is now a regulated profession with the establishment of Care Councils in each of the four UK countries. Social workers are now registered as part of that regulation and required to continue their professional development to ensure re-registration. The Councils have developed Codes of Practice for staff and employees. The Social Care Institute for Excellence was set up at the same time as the Care Councils. Its task is to establish a knowledge base for social care, to develop from that knowledge guidance for policy and practice so that social care is improved - and that improvement is knowledge based.

The emergence of independent social workers is part of this changing world and their numbers are likely to expand. This book makes a very useful contribution to existing practitioners and to those considering independence. It draws on the experience of people working in a range of settings and makes it clear that becoming an 'independent' is not an easy option. The book provides some very practical advice and also relates to the core values of social work. The challenge for independent social workers is to achieve and maintain high standards of practice. To do so they need to have robust arrangements for supervision or mentoring, the commitment to creating time for reflection on their practice and the determination to keep up to date with developing practice.

Social workers work in complex situations. They are often involved in issues where the rights of individuals have to be balanced with society's responsibility to protect - in child protection and mental health, for example. They work with people whose impairments, temporary or permanent, mean that they require support and social care services, without which they are vulnerable. At the heart of social work values are the principles of human rights and social justice. The challenges to work in accordance with these principles in difficult situations are no less for independent social workers.

Bill Kilgallon OBE
Chief Executive
Social Care Institute for Excellence (SCIE)

SCIE's aim is to improve the experience of people who use social care services, by developing and promoting knowledge about good practice in social care. We pull together knowledge from diverse sources through working with a broad range of people and organisations. We share this knowledge freely, supporting those working in social care and empowering service users.

Preface

We would like to thank Bill Kilgallon for taking the time to read the manuscript of this book and to write the Foreword. Bill and his colleagues at the Social Care Institute for Excellence have been generous in their support of the Independents' Forum and have made valued contributions at some of our conferences.

We would also like to take this opportunity to acknowledge and thank the British Association of Social Workers (BASW), which has essentially provided the Independents' Forum with a home during its' growth and development. As the introductory chapter will show, attitudes at BASW towards independent practitioners have changed substantially in the past twenty-five years or so. We look forward to a continuing relationship with the Association and to celebrating the diversity of social work practice in the UK in the decades to come.

This is also a useful opportunity to acknowledge the sustained efforts of the executive committee of the Independents' Forum. Its members willingly give their time to organise events, plan books, convene regional meetings and generally drive the development of the organisation. Somehow, they also find time to work! In particular, we would like to thank all those who were able to contribute a chapter to this publication and for their tolerance of three very focussed editors! As ever, the task was done on time, within specification and with good humour. We hope that you will enjoy the end product.

Gail C. Tucker, Anne Sambidge and Helen Ogilvy

Introduction

Gail C. Tucker

The story so far...

In the 1970s the then recently formed British Association of Social Workers was establishing its ethical position in relation to various aspects of social work practice, in the face of a whole new legislative framework. A working party considered the phenomenon of private social work practice and supported the consensus view at that time, that it was probably not ethical and that the Association should therefore not actively support it. BASW (1979)

Some twenty years and several statutory frameworks later, the same Association started to become very aware of the growing numbers of independent social workers and consultants amongst its own membership. Indeed the UK Chair of the organisation was such a person! With this encouragement it was decided that it was time to respond formally to this very positive development of social work practice.

The first initiative was the launch of a new web-based directory bringing together those BASW members who were working completely independently (not through recruitment agencies) and who wished to use it to promote their services. The intention was to make public access to such services more widely available. This revealed several hundred such members and gave the impetus to plans for an exploratory conference 'Independent Social Work and Consultancy - a professional choice in changing times' to be held in London in March 2001, organised by BASW member Gaynor Wingham in conjunction with BASW and *The Guardian* newspaper. The event was a sell-out success and it established beyond doubt that independent social work was a growing force in the sector and here to stay.

BASW recognised the need for a formal organisation to represent the new entrepreneurial breed of social worker. A small group worked tirelessly to bring about the inaugural conference of the 'Independents' Forum' in Birmingham in June 2002 when the special interest group was officially born.

The rest, as they say, is history. The Forum has grown from strength to strength, with a formal constitution and an active and very effective executive committee, running two events a year for its members and other independent social workers throughout the UK. It has established an authoritative voice on behalf of this small, but significant, group of social work professionals at a key time in the development of the profession, as it has become a registered workforce.

Someone should write a book...

Every week more people contact the committee to enquire about membership, or to seek advice about their own work as an independent practitioner, or just to talk about the possibilities. Recognising the demand, we produced a booklet that pulled together the opinions of many of our members about what it is important to consider when setting up a social work business. This was in its fifth revision when it became clear that there is no real body of literature about this type of social work in the UK, here in the twenty-first century. 'Someone should write a book' was the general conclusion - so we did, and here it is, the first book as far as we are aware, about independent social work and consultancy practice in the UK.

We have set out to introduce you to some of the possibilities and many of the pitfalls of the sector. We do not wish to promote this way of working for the majority, we regard it as a valuable addition to the range of social work provision, which complements public sector social work services and, most importantly, retains a wealth of social work expertise which would otherwise probably have been lost to other professions.

Variety and flair...

As you read the chapters, which have been contributed by members of the Independents' Forum, you will encounter a range of opinions and styles, combining some very serious issues and remarkable creativity. This reflects the very wide cross section of social workers who have elected to run their own businesses and who celebrate the satisfaction they derive from their chosen path. The book is deliberately organised in such a way as to demonstrate the variety of skills along with the qualities and the flair which independent social workers and consultants bring to their work.

Many very experienced social workers reached a point of being unable or unwilling to continue in the increasing bureaucracy of the public sector and could see other ways to deliver services in the new 'market-led' economy. Theirs has been a positive choice.

Social workers first...

In no way do independent social workers and consultants wish to denigrate our colleagues who still work within the public sector services or other employed settings. (Indeed, extensive work in such settings is one of the factors that have helped to equip most independent social workers for their current role.) We celebrate the diversity of social work skills and practice. We are all members of the same profession, sharing the same values and responsible to the same Codes of Practice. We are social workers first and all members of the Independents' Forum are expected to be registered practitioners and to endorse the BASW Code of Ethics. Our primary focus is promoting the highest standards of practice by independent social workers and consultants to the benefit of the people who use their services.

A risky business...?

You will see that independent practice is not a 'soft' option. Stepping outside the security of paid employment and secure pension arrangements is not for the faint hearted. In common with our employed colleagues, we too are working long hours and often enduring personal hardships to do something we believe in. Neither is it necessarily more rewarding financially than employed social work, indeed many report that they 'take home' less pay than previously. Add in uncertainty about where the customers will come from and all the practicalities of running a business and you will see that this is only an option for the most determined to consider.

So why take the risk? The rewards are altogether more intangible and being able to exercise greater control over ones work/life balance to make time for the other priorities in one's life at the same time as being able to exercise professional choice, feature quite prominently in the coming pages.

You may still have questions when you reach the end, in which case we would be delighted to hear from you.

Reference
BASW (1979) *Private Practice in Social Work* BASW Publishing Ltd., Birmingham.

Notes on the contributor
Gail C. Tucker qualified as a social worker in 1975 and practised in local authorities until 1989. She subsequently worked UK-wide and has extensive experience of representing professionals in formal proceedings including tribunals and public inquiries.
Since 1994, Gail has operated her own company as an independent social work consultant and currently acts for several national organisations, advising on Care Standards Act compliance and providing expert witness in the courts.
She is currently Co-Chair of the Independents' Forum, having chaired the organisation since its inception.

Chapter 1

Getting Started

Gail C. Tucker and Colin Luger

This chapter is not exhaustive but aims to provide the reader with some understanding of the issues that an independent social worker or consultant will need to be aware of when starting out.

Expertise

The first thing to consider is what is the 'product' you are going to sell? The demand for services is becoming ever more specialised so spend some time researching amongst your potential customers what it is they need and how this fits with what you can offer. You may be happy to travel for your work or you may prefer to work in a localised area. Attend conferences and seminars and talk to speakers and delegates to build up a picture of the national and local picture. There may be opportunities slightly further afield that you are unaware of. Consider what you have a proven track record in. What are you good at? If you want to branch out, what will be your 'expertise'? What networks do you have? Will you be completely self-employed, employed through an agency, part-time employed or a mixture of all of these?

Personal qualities

If you are going to succeed as an independent social worker, you must be self-confident, able to network and act as a 'stand-alone' professional. Remember, all the credit for a job well done will be down to you, but then so will any mistakes. As you market yourself you will need to have a realistic sense of your value and skills, as well as an ability to be realistic about assessing timescales, setting deadlines, working out costings and saying 'no' when necessary. You will need to be a 'self-starter' with good organisational skills, be a reliable timekeeper with an efficient approach to paperwork, and have some understanding of running a business or be willing to learn. If there is a demand for your services you must be able to maintain an effective work/life balance.

Legal requirements

You should already be registered as a social worker with one of the four Social Care Councils if you have been practising in the UK, (see www.gscc.org.uk), and you may need to have an enhanced Criminal Records Bureau check if you do direct work (check www.crb.gov.uk). Acquaint yourself with the General Social Care Council (GSCC) Codes of Practice (the same wording is used by all four Care Councils). It is advisable to have a mechanism for service-user/employer complaints and feedback. It's the unhappy 'customers' that a business needs to listen to, as well as the satisfied ones.

Supervision/consultation

You will need to be regularly supervised and know where to go if you need consultation on a particular piece of work. It will often be assumed by your customers that you are up-to-date with good practice ideas and thinking. It can reassure enquirers if your CV includes teaching, and if you are offering training. You will also need to ensure that you continue to develop professionally. When you attend an event, ask for a certificate of attendance and keep a log of training undertaken.

Finding customers

The best advertisement for your services is word-of-mouth recommendation from satisfied customers. Once you have carried out quality work, word will get around that you are worth employing, but you have to start somewhere. Draw up a CV or prospectus and circulate it to the organisations who work in the field of your specialism. You may have some very specialised skills that people are crying out for but it may mean you have to travel widely. Members can register on the BASW Independents Online directory of independent social workers and consultants (www.search4socialworkers.com) - each entry is vetted by BASW for compliance with the Code of Ethics. If you decide to set up a website you will need to get your details on to the various search engines and an IT engineer can advise on this.

Business planning and fees

It is helpful to have a business plan, to have an idea of why you are in business, what you are 'selling', where you want to go with the 'product' in the future (six months, a year, two years), and then to review this at least on an annual basis. The outside world will move on very quickly and you will need to take stock and reflect on new challenges and new opportunities.

Do not under estimate your value. If you have specialised skills after years of working in a demanding profession, do not be reluctant to charge what you are worth. You may need to talk to other independent social workers to find out what current fees are but a useful guide is to work out what you would earn in the public sector and add fifty per cent to cover the costs of being self-employed.

Organisational issues

Consider trading under a 'company' name rather than your own name - even as a sole trader. This clarifies your status for Income Tax/National Insurance (NI) purposes. If you trade in your own name alone you will have Tax/NI deductions made from your payments. Or you may prefer to form a partnership with a colleague you trust. An accountant will be able to explain and advise. Consider using a PO Box as your work address if you do not wish to divulge your home address. Consult Royal Mail for more information.

You may choose to set up a limited company. Your accountant will advise on the advantages and disadvantages of this. When choosing a trading name, the Companies House website at www.companieshouse.gov.uk provides information on what you can and cannot name your company. You can also check if a company already exists with the name that you would like to choose.

Keep business administration and records simple. A basic double-entry book-keeping system will be fine. Don't be tempted by software packages unless you are confident in using them. Set time aside at least once a month to deal with issuing invoices, keeping the books straight and chasing up any unpaid invoices. It helps to view the day-to-day business side as part of your work, so build in regular time for it. If you try and fit it in around your professional work it will catch you out eventually and cause stress. Keep a 'to-do' list and review it on a daily basis. If you are running a business you need to be business-like and cash-flow management is critical.

It is well worth appointing an accountant at the start, before you make any mistakes. They will take the worry out of the financial side of your business and will advise you about how to structure the business records and such things as tax returns. It is an idea to ask friends and colleagues for personal recommendations when looking for an accountant. Ask how much they will charge for their services so you don't get any shocks. The issues you will need to be aware of include: how to record your invoices, expenses and mileage, keeping separate bank accounts, capital equipment, Tax and NI, IR35, and possibly VAT. You will need to think about sickness or other forms of lost-income insurance, and a pension. There are specialist organisations who represent small to medium-sized enterprises that are worth joining, as they issue regular bulletins about changes in tax and legislation. Your Local Enterprise Council or Chamber of Commerce can also advise on business start-up.

Contracts

Contracts are the most likely area for disagreements with customers. Make sure that you have written agreements before you commence a piece of work. These can be in the form of a letter which lays out the plan of work, the cost of the work, the timescale, and any conditions. You have as much right to make your terms clear as the organisation employing you. Send two copies and ask the organisation to sign and return one copy to you for your records. If accounts become overdue it is advisable to let them know that you will not be prepared to do any more work until they pay, but this has to be balanced with the needs of the service-user, who must come first.

The bigger the organisation the longer they are likely to take to pay you. State the period within which you expect to be paid on the invoice, for example, 'Terms - Payment within 30 days of date of invoice'. Wherever possible, ask organisations to pay by automatic bank credit, which means that the funds 'clear' more quickly and transaction charges are less. Small businesses can now claim interest on overdue accounts. If you go to www.courtservice.gov.uk and type in 'late payments' in its search engine it will give you relevant information. Don't be afraid to apply interest on late payments and if necessary to pursue through the County Court.

Insurance

You need to inform your buildings and contents insurance provider that your premises are being used as a business. If service users visit your premises you will need to take out public liability insurance. Check that your car insurance covers you for business use, and if you transport service-users, that it specifically covers that activity too. You are strongly advised to have professional indemnity insurance. BASW members can purchase cover as part of their membership but check out the details to make sure your area of work is covered. More and more local authority contracts are requiring evidence of public liability insurance. You should discuss with them the level of 'risk' which they believe your work may incur.

Safety

Personal safety is important as a lone worker. You could leave the address you are going to with a partner or friend with an expected time of your return or you could use a service such as Guardian 24, which uses a mobile telephone to summon help. This is a BASW membership benefit.

Equipment

Consider the benefits of travelling by car or rail - you can work on the train, for example. Have two computers, ideally networked in case one breaks down, and build in regular six-month check-up services. Back up all documents and take steps to make sure any information held electronically or on paper is stored securely. Learn how to access the internet but install an effective anti-virus programme and update it every week; broadband is quicker. A separate business telephone line will save conflict with family members and enable you to 'get away' from the office.

Make sure that you are easily contactable - telephone, fax, answerphone, email and mobile are desirable. Try and keep the same mobile and email address otherwise you will lose business if your customers lose track of you. Be rigorous with your filing and shred every document you discard. If you use an electronic diary, consider using hardcopy 'back-up'. You will be booking work well ahead and your business may be compromised by a computer hardware or software failure.

Personal considerations

Ask yourself whether your family is ready for your change in employment and discuss the practicalities with them. You may think that if you are self-employed you will have complete control of your diary but the reality will be that your customers will dictate the pace. Consider how much of a financial risk you are taking and make sure that you have a cashflow 'buffer' to get you over the initial period whilst you are doing work and waiting for invoices to be paid. Lastly, does this feel the right thing for you to do? Don't ignore your instincts!

Notes on the contributors

Gail C. Tucker qualified as a social worker in 1975 and practised in local authorities until 1989. She subsequently worked UK-wide and has extensive experience of representing professionals in formal proceedings including tribunals and public inquiries.

Since 1994, Gail has operated her own company as an independent social work consultant and currently acts for several national organisations, advising on Care Standards Act compliance and providing expert witness in the courts.

She is currently Co-Chair of the Independents' Forum, having chaired the organisation since its inception.

Colin Luger is a social worker, and a family therapist and systemic practitioner. He has worked in a local authority, the NSPCC, and is currently working independently as an expert in Courts in England and Wales with serious child protection concerns. He is a member of the Independents' Forum of BASW, teaches on the University of the West of England's 'Issues in Child Protection' course and is an honorary family therapist with an NHS Trust.

Chapter 2
Practice Teaching

Colin Biggins

Drawing upon some of my experiences as an independent practice teacher, I intend to offer some useful advice and guidance around issues related to independent practice in this field of work.

Some essential considerations

It is nearly eight years now since I left local government employment in a large Social Services Department to become a self-employed consultant and trainer in social work and social care services. It was a bit of a leap in the dark given that for some time I had worked in fairly senior management roles that had distanced me from frequent direct contact with service users and their families or other practice-based activities. Practice teaching had not really featured in my somewhat sketchy business plan when I decided to become self-employed. Therefore, it was with some trepidation that I agreed to a request from a local university to be the practice teacher for two students who had placements arranged in a day service and a residential setting, but with no suitable (or willing) person on site to take on this role.

Such was the pleading nature of the tutor's request, I could only assume that they were desperate. I was not far wrong. Practice teaching was going through a difficult time in the authority in which the university is located and volunteers were in short supply. The resulting experience, however, was both enjoyable and rewarding (in a non-pecuniary sense) and since that time I have been a practice teacher to more than twenty students from a variety of colleges and universities. From the level of requests that I have received over the years, it would seem that identifying adequate numbers of practice teachers remains problematic. So, if this is an area of work you want to develop, opportunities probably await!

As the degree courses develop and change in the light of the General Social Care Council's (GSCC) information on the new standards in social work training expected during the academic year 2006/07, it is highly likely that courses in England will expect all practice teachers to have gained the GSCC's Practice Teacher Award. For those in the independent sector without the award, gaining it could prove to be problematic without the infrastructure of an employing organisation. Assuming, however, that a place is secured at a local college or university course, then cost might be an issue. If so, it is worthwhile exploring whether the local Regional Post Qualifying Consortium may be able either to make a bursary award or to signpost applicants to other sources of funding. Independent practitioners will also have to arrange to have a mentor external from the academic teaching staff - this could be negotiated with a local authority that has a partnership arrangement with the college or university, although there may be strings attached to this provision. For example, there may be an expectation that you will be practice teacher for their students for a specified period of time after gaining the award! It is also worth bearing in mind that arrangements will need to be made, possibly via your mentor, for at least one practice teaching session to be recorded on video to complement the written part of your course portfolio.

Payments and Contracts

My experience over the last seven years or so is that my reputation (and my availability) has spread by word of mouth and through my profile being available on the BASW Independents Online database (www.Search4SocialWorkers.com). Requests for practice teaching have therefore come from all quarters - from students themselves, from college staff seeking to confirm placement arrangements and, sometimes, from local authority staff development sections working in partnership with a range of courses. Whatever the route, before making a final commitment it is important to be absolutely clear with whom you are contracting to provide this service and who will ultimately be responsible for paying you and at what rate. In the past, I have encountered some difficulties when I have been approached by a college or university who has placed a student in a voluntary sector agency placement. The agency received a payment from the Central Council for Education and Training in

Social Work (CCETSW), as it was then, and included in this was a set daily rate to fund the placement. As the agency may well keep some of the payment for providing the practice placement, do ensure you are clear about what you expect to be paid, including any overheads, such as mileage. For the new one hundred day placements, the GSCC will pay agreed rates per placement to the voluntary and to the statutory sector. With the latter, it may be possible to negotiate an individual rate but for others you will need to negotiate bearing in mind the sum the organisation will receive.

Some practice issues

As an independent practice teacher, you will be carrying out that role on a 'long-arm' basis, with the student having a nominated on-site supervisor who will be responsible for the student's day-to-day work and who will carry case management responsibility. It is extremely important to establish a clear understanding of respective roles and responsibilities when the placement agreement is negotiated - lack of clarity can impede a student's progress and create friction and confusion. Within the placement agreement, issues of confidentiality must be addressed especially in relation to you as practice teacher having access to written case records and meeting service users when observing the student's practice. When roles and relationships are well understood, I have found that the student can really benefit from this three-way relationship, with the on-site supervisor providing support and guidance on the 'mechanics' of the work, as well as the day-to-day contact in monitoring progress. The focus of my input can then be on the actual learning and development taking place within the placement and how well academic teaching is being integrated into practice, for I am a great believer in helping students turn into 'reflective practitioners'.

A word, too, about observations of practice - service users have the right to know who you are and why you are there. Invariably, I have found that the impact of my presence as someone independent from the agency has been an empowering one for the service user. In most cases it appears also to have assisted the professional relationship between service user and student. To quote Smith (2003, p. 12), 'service users may gain confidence from workers involved with them if they see that their practice is regulated and monitored.'

Rewards

Since working independently, practice teaching has been a valuable part of my own work portfolio. The financial rewards of the work can be modest but other rewards include having the opportunities to contribute an independent perspective to the placement experience, to learn about contemporary social work teaching, to build links with universities and colleges and the opportunity to take full advantage of the support offered to practice teachers. In addition, from those links and networks it has certainly been my experience that other exciting and challenging opportunities frequently materialise!

Reference
Smith, M. (2003) *Social Workers Praised by Service Users! What the Climbie Report Doesn't Say.* Practice. 15 (3) pp 7-16

Notes on the contributor
Colin Biggins has worked independently since June 1998, having worked for many years previously in a variety of settings in local authority social services departments. He has a particular interest in mental health and learning disability services and in addition to his work is the secretary of a local mental health charity providing both supported housing and rehabilitation services for those recovering from alcohol dependency.

Chapter 3

Adults with Learning Disabilities

Susan Cheetham

At approximately 9.15am I head to my office at the other end of my house. One of the advantages of working from home is that commuting time tends to be low! My office is a dedicated room furnished with all the necessary office equipment. It is so important to have a work space that one can walk away from at the end of the day, it helps maintain the distinction between work and ordinary life.

The first thing I do is switch on my computer to check the emails (I dread going on holiday as when I return there are hundreds to deal with!). However, this morning isn't too bad - one from an Independents' Forum colleague, the usual financial 'spam' emails, one from my daughter, two from Rachel (my administrative assistant), one from a team manager in Wales and another from a service manager in an English Local Authority. The two emails from Rachel are in connection with a report and an assessment she is typing for me. The one from the team manager is asking if I have time to review an already complex case which appears to be made further complicated by arguments between the home manager and a solicitor about how the service user's Trust Fund should be spent. The service manager has emailed to say that the Local Authority has agreed to my charges to carry out an independent assessment in relation to a married service user with mild learning disabilities who is planning to take the Authority to the High Court if they do not receive the additional services they are requesting.

After responding to the emails I check the list of work I have to do, prioritise and start to tackle the main tasks of the day. Being an independent social worker means that most of my time is spent working in physical isolation, so it is important that I create and maintain a network of support. With this in mind, I contact the associate with whom I liaise closely and from whom I obtain 'peer' supervision. He also advises on the contractual agreements for some of my most complex cases. We discuss one contract and the implications the outcome of my assessment may have for all parties.

He asks if I am available on a certain date as he has to present two mental health reports to the Mental Health Act Managers Hearing but is not free on the date they have arranged. I consult my diary and, as I have no appointments arranged for that date, I agree to attend in his place. He agrees to email me the reports.

I find that time goes very quickly once I get involved in my work and by this time it is now 10.45am.

The telephone rings and it is my contact from the company that provide my IT support. He is due to do his three-monthly visit to check my computer and the anti-virus software in the next week, so we set an appointment.

Back to the tasks in hand, I ruefully remind myself of that time management training I did years ago that said that managing interruptions is the key to success. If only! In the pipeline at the moment is a report for a firm of solicitors in relation to a woman with mental health issues suing a Local Authority. There is also a request for a very thorough NHS and Community Care Assessment and Care Plan as well as a report for a private sector organisation where one of the staff claims that he has been 'bullied' by senior staff. Then there are three Community Care Assessments and two Reviews Reports to be tidied up and just for good measure I need to start preparing a presentation I am giving at a forthcoming conference. I will be sharing a platform with some very well-respected colleagues and I want to be sure I perform well so thorough preparation is essential.

I am just about to launch into my chosen task when the phone rings again. Another call from a Team Manager to say that a service user has been admitted to hospital and the care home Manager has stated that the fee would need to be doubled if she was to return there. Subsequent phone calls to the hospital and a fax from the discharge liaison nurse for Learning Disabilities lead to a phone call to the home Manager and a lengthy debate on the complexity of funding structures. (I spare a thought for colleagues in Local

Authority posts who have to navigate their way through this territory more often than I do). We agree that I will visit the hospital to carry out an assessment. I check my diary for an available date and am reminded that I need to arrange a Guardianship visit with a service user. Both appointments made, I manage to complete the assessments and reviews and photocopy them. This prompts me to add another task to my to-do list - buy another ink cartridge for the photocopier (it seems to be an unspoken law of the universe that to-do lists grow rather than shrink). One of the challenges of working independently is that one has to take responsibility for all aspects of the business, from paper clips to contracts, from toner for the photocopier to tone of the organisation and all points in between. Self-reliance and good organisational skills are a must.

It is now 2.20pm and time for some lunch. It is a late lunch today as I am expecting a visit from a builder to confirm the details of some work. Another skill of working from home lies in managing the boundaries between work and ordinary life. Whilst it is convenient to be able to arrange such appointments to fit around work commitments, one sometimes has to remind people that one is not free to socialise - but there's always time for a cup of tea! The other practical issue is ensuring that people who call at the house, whether by appointment or not, do not have access to the office or see any confidential material.

I get back into the office at 2.55pm and check the emails - nothing significant and decide that I will start my presentation as I have at least an hour in hand before I need to leave for my last appointment of the day.

At 4.15pm I stop writing, check the emails and lock the paperwork away. With the office properly secured, it is time to take the parents of a young man with Learning Disabilities to look at a potential placement as the care home where he lives is closing. Due to their work commitments his parents are only available at evenings and weekends. For me, one of the benefits of being an independent social worker is flexibility. Tonight I do not need to use my Guardian 24 system for lone workers as I know the parents quite well, but it is a comforting asset to have when doing an initial visit to someone I have not met before.

I am also a long-distance tutor for a college running a Dementia Awareness course and on my return home have to telephone a Learner to discuss a question she has stated she needs support with.

Today, my working day ends at nearly 9pm and I make the transition back to domestic life. Physically, it isn't a long journey home, it is only down the hall - but psychologically, the transition is important and made easier by doing something to relax and focus my mind elsewhere, even if it is only having an hour with my feet up watching a favourite television programme.

Notes on the contributor
Susan Cheetham trained as a nurse and managed residential care homes for older people before qualifying as a social worker at the University of the West of England. After working in various Hospital Social Work posts, in a Disabled Adults Team and a Learning Disabilities Team she became an independent social worker in 2003. She combines being a long-distance tutor and marker of papers on Dementia Awareness with her main work on challenging cases in the Learning Disabilities field.

Chapter 4

Direct Work with Children:
The Land of Possibility

Valerie Childs

When I was first asked to contribute the 'children's voice' to this book I felt scared. How does one contribute to the whole without knowing the other parts? What do I know about writing book chapters? I'm just a childcare social worker.

A voice inside asked, 'What are you afraid of?' and I thought, 'I'm so busy, so much to do, if I do that I can't do…'. Eventually a gentle internal monologue began. It spoke about fear of not fitting in, fear of failure, fear of the unknown. I was conscious of smiling to myself, wasn't this the same conversation I'd had with myself when thinking about becoming an independent social worker? It's all about taking risks!

I thought about children I have worked with who have had terrifying experiences at the hands of adults, but who risk time and time again their entire beings in a humbling spirit of optimism.

Risk is a curious word, it can either mean all things hazardous or all that is possible. In my work as an independent social worker, I have had negative experiences, but these are outweighed by the positives. The possibilities I have encountered, promoted, invented and participated in have been exciting, invigorating and have refuelled the ideals that drew me to this work some thirty years ago.

This said, throughout my career I have met and continue to meet dedicated and gifted local authority childcare social workers - there is need of both.

Becoming an independent social worker has afforded me the opportunity of being differently involved in childcare social work.

I believe it is the broad spectrum of work that expands my practice, knowledge and expertise.

For example, in a week I'll see a four-year-old subject of Care Proceedings who is having night terrors and give telephone support to an adoptive parent post Order, before visiting a bereaved family. I'll work with a fifteen-year-old who can't speak, but who will share their innermost fears and I'll plan the evaluation of a new University Diploma. I'll undertake workers' supervision and lead groups for parents and children and an evening group for teenagers. I'll attend a business meeting as the Chair of a Joint Fostering and Adoption Panel and finish the evaluation of a schools anti-bullying project. I'll draft a new organisational policy and agree to sit on another committee. I'll also attend to administration tasks and take various phone calls - some regarding existing work and some to discuss new business.

By the end of the week I'll have travelled several hundred miles by car, bus, train and tube and worked for self-referred people, local authorities, charities, private and voluntary agencies, the police and children's and adults education providers. If I had not risked trying the path of independence, I would have missed so many opportunities.

Child Care social workers and the children they work with take risks all the time. I hope the following story illustrates some multi-level risk taking. I chose to write it in 'fairy tale' form as a tribute to the children and families who have risked working with me.

Once upon a time there was a Woman who had travelled for more than two-and-a-half decades in the Same Land. She had met lots of Nice People, some Not So Nice People and many many, Special Children - for her, this was the Best Part of the journey.

On her travels the Woman had had to carry Papers and listen to Big People talking. One day she realised she was carrying so many Papers and spending so much time listening to Big People talking that she no longer saw the Special Children and this made her very sad.

The Woman began to see she could no longer stay in the Same Land, but knew she still wanted to continue the journey. She looked at a few Other Places and eventually decided she wanted to go to the Land of Independence.

The Woman has had many quests during five years in the new Land. She still has to carry some Papers (but not many) and sometimes listen to Big People talking (but not often). The Woman has met more Nice People and more Not So Nice people. However, she spends most of her time with Special Children and she works in Different Places and does lots of Different Things.

One day the Woman was told about a Little Boy who needed a New Family. To try and help him understand why this was so, the Big People asked the Woman who knew about these things to go and see the Little Boy.

After many weeks the Little Boy began to understand and although it made him feel sad, he started to look forward to the New Family being found.

The Big People asked the Woman to help them look for this New Family. The Woman found a New Family and after a time they went to meet the Little Boy. Everyone was happy and excited. After some more meetings the Little Boy went to live with the New Family. The Woman still went to see him, to help the Little Boy and the New Family to learn how to live together.

In the beginning the Little Boy and the New Family each had Someone of their own who was also helping with everything, but after a very little while, both the Someones went away and no new ones could be found.

One day the Woman got a telephone call from the Big People. She was told never to see or talk to the Little Boy, his New Family or Other People ever again!

The Woman didn't understand and didn't know what to do; she was very upset. She decided to tell Other People what had happened because she was so worried - the Little Boy and the New Family would wonder what had happened when she didn't visit and they wouldn't know why, and they no longer had Someone to help them either. The Woman knew she would probably get into lots of trouble and the Big People might never speak to her again, but she was more worried about the Little Boy and his New Family because they were still learning how to live together.

Other People were shocked this had happened. They told the New Family. The New Family was very, very angry and upset. They quickly wrote a very long letter to the Big People and telephoned them. The New Family were very wise and they used Magic Words in their letter and on the telephone - words like Statutory Responsibility; Legal Advice; Complaints Procedure.

The Magic Words made the Big People try and find out what had happened. After a while the Big People sorted out the muddle, said sorry to the New Family and the Woman but, sadly, not to the Little Boy. The New Family and the Woman decided to pretend that the Big People wanted the Little Boy to know they were sorry and this made him feel better.

The Big People then asked the Woman if she would carry on helping the Little Boy and the New Family for another whole year. She said she would and everyone is trying to live happily ever after.

The Woman has found the Land of Independence littered with risk but also opportunity:

- risk to children's plans but the opportunity to speak out independently
- risk to children's futures but the opportunity to challenge and to creatively develop service provision
- risk to reputation and ethics but the opportunity to determine whether a commission is sustainable
- risk to values but the opportunity to reinforce good practice standards
- risk to income but the opportunity to maintain professional integrity - priceless!

For me, independent social work is indeed a risky business - fraught with magical possibilities.

Notes on the contributor

Valerie Childs' unbroken childcare social work career began in 1976. She holds a range of professional and academic qualifications. Her BSc in Social Work (First Class Honours) included studying at a Child and Family Consultation Service (C&FCS) facility attached to St John's University, Newfoundland. Her dissertation on the development of group work programmes for families surviving domestic violence was published. She achieved her Post-Graduate Diploma in Systemic Family Therapy at the Tavistock Clinic, London and is a qualified trainer. She is currently completing her MA (Practice) under the new GSCC awards scheme. Valerie has been working independently for five years.

Chapter 5

Interim Management

Tim Gretton

In writing this chapter I am grateful to my colleague Malcolm Whitehead, who also operates a company providing interim management, who has contributed to some of the ideas covered.

What is an Interim Manager?

I have it on good authority that it may have been Enzo Ferrari, founder of the motor-racing organisation, who said that all committees should be made up of an unequal number of people...and three's too many.

If you want something done on time, on budget and which works effectively, don't use a committee, get the right person for the job. At short notice or in an emergency, that will be the Interim Manager.

There are a couple of myths that should be dispelled straight away:

- Independent Interim Managers do that work because of redundancy and probably don't have the same commitment as permanent staff.
- Managers of more mature years don't have the dynamism to turn around troubled projects.

These are not evidenced by the rapid expansion of interim management agencies in recent years. The expansion is fuelled by the demand by local authorities and other organisations, which are being required to develop and deliver more effective, more efficient and more responsive services within tight timescales. They require highly skilled and experienced managers, at short notice, to troubleshoot and build the firm foundations for future developments whilst other recruitment processes are followed.

What do Interim Managers actually do?

Well, almost anything, from being an area office team manager to a director - and you may find yourself working at very different levels in the hierarchy on different assignments. For instance, I have worked as a senior manager of a private fostering agency, a programme manager for a large children's voluntary organisation and a team manager for a Supporting People team. Did I say that flexibility and versatility were requirements for the work? It really is all about transferable skills.

Is it for me?

It is not necessary to be quite as versatile as this and some Interim Managers choose to operate at a particular level, say team manager, which suits their skills, experience and comfort level in respect of challenge.

A useful rule in the early days is not to take on an assignment above a level that you have worked at previously. And this is often the rule that commissioning organisations will be working to as well. They really do expect Interim Managers to 'hit the ground running' and they will want to be confident that you have the requisite skills and experience.

It is a necessary pre-requisite of becoming an Interim Manager that you have risk-assessed your strengths and areas for development. You will need to find the right balance between challenge, professional development and over-reaching yourself. It is better to say 'No' occasionally to a request that you are not confident of fulfilling than risk losing the confidence of the commissioning organisation.

How do I go about it?

Most local authorities automatically think of agencies when needing to source Interim Managers and in the early days it may be helpful to register with one or two until you get yourself known and your other marketing strategies start to kick in. There are many advertisements in the trade press and some national newspapers.

What are the key skills that you will need to have?

In common with descriptions of other independent social work roles these will include:

- Confidence in your own knowledge and skills.
- Ability to analyse complex organisations and situations quickly and accurately.
- Quick relationship building.
- Ability to transfer knowledge and skills from one setting to another.
- 'Business objectives' focus.
- Project and change management skills.
- Ability to identify strengths in staff and utilise them quickly.
- Ability to take care of yourself amidst processes of change.

Your ability to analyse complex organisations and situations quickly will prove especially interesting and challenging, and will improve as you move from one contract to another. One month you may be working for a small organisation that has few management structures in place but where the making of far-reaching decisions, followed by implementation, can be completed in a matter of days. Next month you may be working for a local authority where the same decision-making processes may take many months and the monitoring of consistent implementation of changes is a far greater challenge. Your next contract may be for a large organisation that has national policies and procedures but where the level of local management autonomy is high. Whatever the situation, you will need to be clear about the structures, dynamics and expectations within that particular organisation, as this understanding will have a direct bearing on how best to approach the task.

As a consequence of this variety, Interim Managers have wide experiences and depth of knowledge from many organisations to bring with them and this is one of the resources that commissioning organisations are purchasing from you. You must be able to stand back from the organisation and group dynamics and be confident to say how it really is. The fact that an Interim Manager was required will usually indicate that the organisation is experiencing significant difficulties. Constructive, honest analysis and well-reasoned developments will be welcomed with open arms and introducing new systems that actually work and deliver effective, efficient services, even more so.

Interim management is usually focused on managing change, so you will need to be especially confident in your management of change skills and knowledge. In order to change organisations quickly, as a newcomer, people need to trust you so you can take them with you. Tell them where they are going, why, how they are going to get there and finally, how to recognise when they have arrived.

Location and looking after yourself

You need a clear idea about where you are prepared to work, based upon your personal circumstances. Depending on your target area for work, you may be asked to relocate at fairly short notice, although it is also surprising how far you may be prepared to travel to work to avoid the prospect of unreliable temporary accommodation! If you are working through an agency, initially, it is likely that you will be approached to consider work over a wide area and staying away from home may be the only option. In addition to hotels and bed & breakfast accommodation, you should also consider holiday accommodation such as caravans, cottages and flats (particularly in the low season).

Most organisations will consider Interim Managers working for three-four days a week, so it is possible to manage the time away to an extent and include other work closer to home during the rest of the week. At one time I didn't follow my own advice and travelled a return journey of one hundred and sixty miles South for two days each week and spent the rest of my working week staying away in a city some two hundred miles north of my home. It was not an altogether happy time, so please learn from my experience!

What are the risks and how do you assess them?

The one I am most conscious of is being confident that I am able to meet the targets in the contract. I use a checklist to address this:

- Have I done this type of work before?
- Have I done something similar before?
- What do I need to learn to complete this work successfully?
- Can I complete the majority of this learning in, say, two weeks?

The contract in respect of managing a Supporting People project was one where this risk assessment was most difficult to complete, due to the complexity and ever-changing nature of the work and of the expectations flowing from the Office of the Deputy Prime Minister. Nevertheless, the authority moved from one to two stars whilst I was there, so you can draw your own conclusions!

Some organisations will insist that Interim Managers have their own liability insurance, whilst others provide this cover and this must be explicitly agreed at the outset. BASW membership brings with it professional indemnity cover, which covers your individual practice as a social worker in respect to errors or omissions but public liability for an Interim Manager needs separate cover.

In conclusion

What are the most important messages to hang on to?

- Find time to think and reflect.
- Insist on a clear brief, check it is consistent with your business plan, and stick to it.
- If you start to be treated like a regular member of staff, you may be losing your interim management impact. It's time to move on...

Notes on the contributor

Tim Gretton is director of Woodlands Group, a social work and management consultancy. Previously he was director of a residential childcare company. Tim has offered interim management services since 2003, working for a number of organisations as troubleshooter and strategic advisor, implementing appropriate management systems and supporting their CSCI registration. Tim also provides childcare consultancy services and has recently extended his skills by designing and implementing a Supporting People review programme. He is studying for a Leadership in Social Care qualification.

Chapter 6

The Risks Under My Roof

Meral Mehmet

There are days when risk never crosses your mind although, subconciously, you are probably analysing it all the time. Then there are those days when risk just slaps you in the face - as the following account of one twenty-four hour period in my life shows only too clearly!

4.00pm
After spending all day putting finishing touches to a complex report, I email it across before the agreed deadline of 5.30pm. As I'm doing so it occurs to me just how much I - and all the other independent social workers I am in contact with - have come to rely upon the internet, particularly the email system, to support our work.

4.15pm
I receive confirmation from the organisation who commissioned my report that they have received it safely. I am relieved that the time-consuming, quite complicated pieces of work which culminated in this final report were completed on time and to a standard I can be proud of. As I feel drained by the effort that has gone into ensuring this I decide not to spend any more time at my desk or in front of my computer today. Instead, I plan that my first task tomorrow will be to back up all the work I've done on the computer over the past three weeks leading up to the completion of today's report.

9.00pm
Having spent a couple of hours out of the house, I arrive home - alone - to find I've interrupted two burglars in the very act of ransacking my house! I don't know who is more surprised. Fortunately, the intruders don't hang about, legging it through my back door even as I collect my wits. I take a very

quick look around, taking great care not to disturb anything, to see what damage they might have done. It seems to me as though my unwelcome visitors had broken the bathroom window before wending their way through upstairs, picking through things as they went until they reached my office.

As I scan the chaos that now exists in my office it is immediately obvious that the burglars have had a field day. In addition to some personal items, my entire PC, keyboard, speakers and printer have all been stolen! And along with these, the main means both of my livelihood and of the way I communicate with my network of work contacts has also been been stolen.

9.05pm Highly relieved to find that my office telephone lines are not only intact but also still working I ring 999. I am told the police will come as soon as they can.

Meanwhile, I make other telephone calls to alert my husband and family. Whilst waiting their arrival I notice my diary still in my office. I also see that my most recently updated computer disk is in its usual place. Even though I am in a state of shock it occurs to me that these items alone might mean that I will be able to hold work things together in the immediate aftermath of the burglary.

11.00pm When the police appear they are polite but pessimistic. They advise that I should disturb as little as possible overnight until 'scene of crime officers' can visit but this won't be until tomorrow.

My husband arrives back at this stage. He points out that his laptop is still resting on his desk so questions whether his was not good enough to steal. We joke about having had discerning thieves in order to ward off the other, very real, probability that my return home disturbed the intruders before they could escape with that computer, too. My husband

and I are slightly consoled by the thought that at least his work and his livelihood have not been affected by the break-in.

2.00am I go to bed and immediately go straight to sleep, exhausted by the events of the day.

4.00am I come to suddenly with 'what if' questions buzzing around my head: what if the burglary had happened the previous day and I hadn't already forwarded the report I'd spent so much time working upon? What if all that work had been lost? What if I hadn't backed up the work I had done? What if I hadn't kept receipts to prove that I had all the office equipment? What if I hadn't got adequate insurance to cover all my losses? What if I hadn't available a 'tried and tested' computer specialist whom I will be able to call upon immediately to support me to find the right machine and type of programmes to enable me to return to work and normalcy within the next few days? I have work I need to complete and strict deadlines to uphold.

Fully awake by now, this sets me thinking about the myriad risks under my roof, particularly how important it is for any independent social worker to have a business continuity plan that would operate in the event of such a burglary. Vowing to pay more specific attention to this in the daytime, I finally drift into a fitful sleep.

10.45am Uncertain how best to go on until the promised 'scene of crime officers' have paid their visit, I am relieved when they arrive quite early in the day. As they go about their work I discover another of the casualties from my office - my passport has been stolen. This causes me consternation not just because of the obvious inconvenience of having to replace it but also because I have been asked to produce it for a police check in connection with a new piece of work for an organisation I haven't worked for previously.

11.15am   Whilst the police are still busy in the house I make a series of phone calls and discover that the Criminal Records Bureau is prepared to accept an original birth certificate (one that is obtained around the time of a person's actual birth). This means I will be able to complete the form without the passport so there will not be any delay over the start of the new contract.

11.45am   After discussion first with the police and then with my insurers they readily agree that I can go ahead and buy the vital equipment I need to get me back and working just so long as I keep any receipts to support my insurance claim. As I have routinely kept all receipts for equipment purchased for my office I am assured that I will be able to get my investment back. I immediately make plans with my IT specialist for the purchase of a new computer system.

4.00pm   Just twenty-four hours after feeling so elated about a job well done, I begin to put together the beginnings of a formal business continuity plan, which will need further refining in the days and weeks that follow - to store hard copies of important documents safely; to ensure confidential material is shredded if no longer needed; to continue to be rigorous about work documents being securely locked away; to avoid keeping important personal documents together in the same place in order to prevent them being easily removed in one fell swoop. Most particularly, to ensure that all work done on the computer is always routinely and regularly backed up and with the back-up copy stored off site. That will mean that in the event of any other unforeseen event a return to business with as little interruption as possible can take place speedily, leaving my reputation and integrity completely intact.

As I complete this list it occurs to me that whilst I wouldn't wish a burglary upon anyone, it has demonstrated just how easily an independent social worker's business can be put at risk.

Notes on the contributor

Meral Mehmet has worked in social services for over twenty-one years since obtaining her CQSW and DipSW. She has worked in the children's sector, latterly specialising in fostering.

She has worked as an Independent Consultant for the past five years and is the author of a recent book regarding Fostering Standards. She has also contributed to another publication on fostering.

Chapter 7

Independent Social Work and Adoption

Pam Norrington

Adoption work is a specialist area within Family Placement social work. The national shortfall in social workers combined with simultaneous pressures on agencies to meet various targets - recruitment of adopters, numbers of children placed, new responsibilities for adoption support enshrined in the Adoption and Children Act (2002) - provides opportunities for work for independent adoption and fostering social workers like myself.

What are the risks in undertaking independent adoption work?

Business risks

- Work may be intermittent if assessments or commissions are taken singly. Alternatively, negotiating a contract for a series of assessments can mean lower rates of remuneration or a 'fixed fee'.
- Adoption work involving reviews, complaints, research projects or writing policies/procedures is usually a 'one-off' commission. Carefully consider whether you can *accurately* estimate the hours of work. I undertook an adoption support research project for which a fixed fee was agreed - the hours of research were accurately estimated but not the report writing which took considerably longer!
- The independent worker runs the risk of work 'drying up' when staff vacancies are filled, staff become fully trained or the 'funds' run low. There will always be 'difficult' assessments where there are 'issues' but their regularity cannot be guaranteed. Diversification into other areas is advisable!

Practice Risks

- In terms of professional liability, I would suggest that the risks in undertaking independent adoption work are relatively low in comparison with some other social work tasks. Adoption assessments provide a *recommendation* subject to the scrutiny of an adoption panel. Adoptive applicants are partners in this process with recourse to the adoption agency's complaints procedure as well as the Independent Review Mechanism. I am not yet aware of any scenario whereby applicants or the agency have held an assessor professionally liable for a recommendation, disrupted placement, or for an applicant later found to be 'unsuitable'.
- Independent social workers who act as adoption panel members are similarly part of the shared decision-making process and subject to review by the agency.
- Adoption support work can be more open to liability depending on the nature of the work and commission, for example if the adopted adult or birth parent is considered a 'risk' to other parties. However, a risk assessment combined with advice from the independent consultant and respecting of accepted protocols should minimise liability.
- Risk is always reduced when the social worker practises in an area of expertise, so when venturing into a new area, ensure adequate consultation and training. Recently I was asked to undertake an inter-country adoption, but declined. I have insufficient experience in this field and insufficient time at present to arrange specialist consultation or research.
- In general, taking on too many assessments can lead to obvious difficulties of workload balance/inattention to detail.

What are the responsibilities?

Responsibilities are threefold:

- Ensuring that service users in the adoption cycle are provided with a highly professional service in which they are fully involved.
- Negotiating a clear, realistic contract with the commissioner and undertaking the task as agreed, reviewing any changes over timescales or task.

- Maintaining professional standards within the adoption field, recognising the shared responsibility for Looked After Children.

What are the key skills?

In addition to good organisational skills, self-discipline and experience, adoption work requires:

- Extensive knowledge of fostering and children and families statutory work.
- Familiarity with fostering and adoption legislation and regulations.
- Knowledge of how adoption panels function.
- Experience in the whole 'cycle' of adoption work from preparation and assessment of applicants, matching, linking and moving children on, individual work and life-story work with children, contact with birth families, adoption support, through to counselling of adopted adults and birth families.
- Expertise in the assessment of adoption applicants (utilising, for example, the Form F format produced by British Agencies for Adoption and Fostering).
- Awareness of attachment, loss and trauma, the importance of identity and self-esteem and the relevance of these for the adoptive task, especially for the development of resilience in the child.

Practice issues for independent adoption workers

The practice issues relate to both service users and commissioner and also to how the independent worker interfaces with an existing agency.

- Continuity of support for the service user may not be possible, for example when the contract is to undertake just the adoption assessment or only the initial interview in birth-record counselling. Such limitations require a clear explanation to the service user at the outset of the work.
- There are different procedural processes in different organisations. For example, who is responsible for references? What else might be required in addition to the Form F for the adoption panel? What is the organisation's process for linking

adopters with children? Who undertakes the direct work with children? Developing helpful links with staff in the adoption agency will ease your path.

- There needs to be agreement about the documentation the commissioning agency will provide for the independent social worker and a commitment from the independent worker to adhere to the regulations, such as keeping adoption files safely locked in a fire-proof cabinet.
- There may be unexpected outcomes from an independent adoption assessment. For example, where a child is already known to the applicants, adoption could be an expedient solution. An adverse independent assessment may cause difficulties for that agency and might result in pressure upon the assessor to 'modify' the assessment. In such situations the independent worker needs to consider carefully how to progress such a situation in order to retain professional integrity.
- There is a need to balance having work (and income!) with taking on too many commissions and assessments. Competitive tendering situations may tempt the independent social worker to quote or agree unrealistic timescales, affecting quality of work and limiting the time adoptive applicants have for reflection and preparation for the task. It is important, too, to work within one's own comfort zone but also to embrace new challenges and skills.
- The main problem in this area of work, as with any other independent social work, can be a lack of a 'team' for support and alternative opinions. It is essential, therefore, to establish an arrangement for this, perhaps through peer consultation or by undertaking contracts in partnership with an independent colleague.

Conclusions

Independent social workers can be involved in direct work throughout the whole adoption 'cycle', from recruitment of new adopters through the matching and placement process, to counselling adult adopted persons and their families. Development of birth-parent counselling and adoption support responsibilities may afford further opportunities for independent practitioners. Indirect work can involve writing policies and procedures, being involved in specialised projects, chairing adoption panels or being a member of an adoption panel. In my experience, a wide range of adoption work is available for the independent social worker with sufficient specialist knowledge to undertake it, although in some locations there may not be sufficient work to sustain full-time hours on adoption work alone. However, adoption work can often be successfully combined with fostering commissions, with kinship work or with direct work with children.

Some of the 'pitfalls' of working independently have been outlined above, others have been identified elsewhere in this book. The rewards? The tremendous variety of work at all times plus the opportunity of gaining and utilising best practice from a variety of adoption agencies.

Note: The implementation in England of the Adoption and Children Act 2002 at the end of 2005 has led to debate whether professionals producing independent adoption assessment reports and/or adoption counselling services should be separately registered as Adoption Support Agencies or whether they are covered by the registration of the authority which commissions their work.

There have been different interpretations of the legislation in various parts of the country and the matter remains unresolved at the time of going to press.

You are advised to take individual advice if you are involved in such work.

Notes on the contributor

Pam Norrington graduated from Bath University in 1975. She has worked for Local Authorities in a variety of posts ranging from children and families' teams, child psychiatry and child guidance to fostering and adoption.

Pam has been an independent social worker since October 2001, specialising in adoption and fostering work of all kinds in the West Midlands, Worcestershire and Gloucestershire.

Chapter 8

Working with Adults

Helen Ogilvy

Whilst Noel Coward (1931) may well have been right in his assertion that 'mad dogs and Englishmen go out in the midday sun', surely social workers and care managers in adult services don't venture out into the unpredictable climate of independent social work and consultancy? Surely it is much safer to remain in more traditional settings, where the climate, if not ideal, is at least reasonably predictable?

A growing minority of professionals disagree. On an average week, the Independents' Forum receives three or four enquiries from qualified social workers who are considering making the transition to independent practice - around half are currently care managers or senior managers in adult services. Whilst some test out the idea and decide that the right decision for them is to remain where they are or seek a different post, many find that when they weigh up the pros and cons, the risks are fewer than they initially imagined. For some, the risks of making that transition are less than the personal and professional risks of remaining where they are.

So in what areas of work with adults do people find a temperate niche? What are some of the risks they manage and what are some of the benefits?

Areas of work

As evidenced in some of the other chapters of this book, colleagues in children's services have found a wide variety of niches where independent practice can flourish. The same is true in adult services, as the following list illustrates:

- Assessment of an individual service user's, or carer's, needs. This might happen in situations where a complaint has been made and there is a need for an independent opinion. It might happen in situations where people are funding their own care and want independent professional advice rather than approaching the local authority.

- Consultation exercises with service users and carers (and with professionals too). This might occur when the future shape of services is up for debate and there is a need for an independent person to conduct this in a transparent way.
- Advocacy, with groups or with individuals. One independent social worker I spoke with last year spends part of his time using the medium of photography as an advocacy tool in working with adults with communication difficulties - evidence that with imagination, one can create some highly specialised niches.
- Reviews or evaluations of services, perhaps when funding is up for renewal and some judgement is required as to whether the service has achieved what it set out to achieve and whether there are any issues to be resolved.
- Advice and representation work, for example with service providers where there is a dispute with the purchaser or with social workers who find themselves in conflict with employers on professional matters.
- Interpreting policy and advising organisations around translating the policy intent into good practice in their domain.
- Expert witness and other para-legal work.
- Training and staff development work, particularly in the wake of new developments in law, policy and practice.

Risks

In all these areas of work, there are inherent risks - both business and professional. You have to achieve a balance between having in-depth knowledge of a topic and maintaining a breadth of interest - strategically, it does not make sense to box yourself into a highly specialised corner, particularly if a change in policy might wipe that corner off the map. You also have to maintain a range of potential sources of work as there is the risk that some sources will dry up from time to time. Alternatively, you may want to distance yourself if your professional position has been compromised. Many people worry that by clearly stating their independent professional opinion there is a risk of alienation from a customer or potential customer. It is certainly the case that tact and diplomacy are standard tools of the trade for independent social workers and consultants but, by and large, customers value the independent view, as long as it is clearly evidenced.

There are also risks associated with over-stretching yourself, either in the nature of the work or the volume of work undertaken. It is important to be clear about what you are good at and how much you can realistically do in a given timeframe. Particularly in the early days of a business, the temptation is to take anything on that comes along - it takes a great deal of discipline to say no at appropriate times, either because you do not have the appropriate knowledge and skills or because you do not have sufficient time to do justice to the work. However, this discipline is important as reputation is built on results and can be lost rather more quickly than built. As always, though, it is easier to preach the concept than demonstrate it!

Another potential risk is that of professional isolation - independence can be a lonely furrow to plough and it is important to build in opportunities to discuss professional issues, exchange ideas and generally find the support that team structures to some extent can provide. One of the benefits of the Independents' Forum is the development of such networks, if people want to take advantage of the opportunities.

Benefits

As we know from our professional practice, on the whole, risks can be managed and minimised if you are aware of them. For many people, one of the benefits of independent practice lies in being able to take full responsibility for risks and to adopt a positive approach to risk, rather than the defensive stance that they often found in their employing organisation. Many independent practitioners I have spoken to find that being able to take responsibility for risk in their practice enables them to work more fully within the spirit of the Codes of Practice and within the BASW Code of Ethics, enabling others to make informed choices.

Perhaps one of the greatest benefits of practising independently, whether within adults or children's services, lies in being able to take effective control of your Post-Registration Training and Learning. Independent practice gives the opportunity to weave the strands of the work you enjoy into a portfolio that reflects your interests and expertise - a portfolio in which the components complement and inform each other. As an independent social worker or consultant, it is important to build in time for your own training and development and to cost that into your fee structure.

So, getting back to predictable climates, the reality is that the climate in the world of independent social work and consultancy is probably no less predictable than that in more traditional settings. (Indeed, the climate in these more traditional settings is itself going through substantial change.) It is, however, a climate where most professionals who have made the move feel they have greater control over the way the wind blows and the direction they can set for their journey. Whilst not right for everyone, it has become the climate of choice for a growing group of professionals. Mad dogs? I don't think so!

Reference
Coward, N. (1931) *Mad dogs and Englishmen*. Collected Sketches and Lyrics. Hutchinson, London.

Notes on the contributor
Helen Ogilvy has been actively involved in the health and social sectors since graduating from St Andrews University, Scotland with an honours degree in Psychology in 1980. She is a qualified social worker (University of Wales, 1985) and has worked within both the statutory and voluntary sectors.
She has been an independent consultant and trainer since 1994, specialising in community care issues. She is currently Co-Chair of the Independents' Forum.

Chapter 9
All In A Day's Work

Eddie O'Hara

In the world of independent social work there are times when professional doors open, close, and sometimes revolve so quickly that they hit you in the back before you are safely through to the other side and the opportunity is gone forever.

As my colleagues in other parts of this book have so clearly illustrated, above all else independent social work is not for those generally seeking an easier life. It is a world where only those with a clear sense of professional identity, integrity and a sense of humour survive.

What is a working day like for me? Before I begin, I would point out that almost by definition, 'my day' as an independent social worker is probably nothing like any of my colleagues', except perhaps that collectively we at least have some control over our professional lives in making a positive difference to the lives of others. A big claim perhaps, but nonetheless true for making it.

So here goes!

6.00am   Put the dog out and check my emails.
             A colleague in Canada has emailed me his most recent article on 'separated parents' and a senior manager in a local authority has asked if I can send her some information, which she needs first thing. As an independent social worker based at home, not only are you able to keep in touch with various colleagues who also work long, flexible hours, you are also able to keep up to speed with daily government briefings via email.

6.15am   Whilst cycling around the park with my dog (I should point out that he runs, I cycle) I consider the coming day and remind myself that today I am going to work smarter, not harder.

7.00am   Kiss my partner, wake my children, feed the dog and check my emails. By this time many of my fellow independent social workers are already emailing each other like 'people possessed', before they set forth on their current daily endeavours. Like it or not in the world of independent social work, the early bird usually does get the worm.

7.15-8.00am   Me time!

8.00am   Check my emails and sort through the post.
Yet again, despite assurances from a solicitor yesterday that the court papers will be with me today, the court papers for another so-called 'urgent' assessment fail to arrive on time. I'll have to inform the solicitor later today that if the bundle isn't here by tomorrow, we may need to postpone the final hearing. That should get things moving!

8.30am   Set my office telephone to 'divert' and head off for my first assessment session of the day.

11.00am   Finish assessment session. Check for telephone messages and emails on my new state-of-the-art mobile phone, which, to be honest, I can barely switch on.

12.30pm   Present an adoption case to a local authority adoption panel. Panel agree with my recommendation, family happy, I'm relieved!

1.15pm   Check for telephone messages and emails and telephone solicitor about those court papers.

1.20pm   Telephone call from a family cancelling today's 3.00pm appointment as they have decided they no longer want to be considered as carers for a distant nephew. Good decision by the family, even though my accountant will count the loss of another cancelled session.

1.40pm   Meeting with the co-ordinator of a social work training course who thought I might be able to contribute. As the co-ordinator fills out some unrelated paperwork (in my time) they explain what they want from me, which, by the way, I'm expected to do at a reduced fee on the basis of it being 'a great honour to be asked'.

Suffice to say that on leaving, I have a clearer insight into why some academic institutions struggle so hard to get experienced practitioners to contribute to their courses. Not for me, I'm afraid!

2.30pm   Re-arrange diary and return to the office. Begin writing up a report, which is not due for completion for a few weeks.

3.30pm   A solicitor telephones to enquire if I can assess a birth parent whose child is in foster care, and if so, can he have a proposal and my current CV by the end of the day. It appears the local authority is refusing to assess his client, and the case is back in court first thing in the morning.

I agree to get a proposal and CV faxed to him by first thing tomorrow. Strange how many solicitors are not yet online.

I begin to have second thoughts about committing an hour putting together the proposal when I know the odds of a late/unplanned enquiry coming to anything are usually less than 15:1.

Still I console myself with nothing ventured...nothing gained.

4.00pm	Check my emails. I notice a request has been made for a Turkish-speaking independent social worker to carry out an urgent assessment. I pass the enquiry on to a Turkish colleague.
	Coming through on the emails I notice that there's a lot of talk about the transitional arrangements for the Children Act (2002). Time to check out if my next legal course covers the new requirements. It does.
	Make a few telephone calls to local authority colleagues about various ongoing cases. Many of them are out on child protection investigations. Those were the days... actually, who am I kidding! Several of them are on sick leave.
4.45pm	Check my emails. Regular as clockwork, 'info4local.gov.uk' emails me with all the latest government departmental press releases, publications, and so on. I'm spoilt for choice about whether I should read up on BSE, Young Offenders or the rise in Chlamydia ... I think I'll settle for a cup of tea!
5.45pm	I fax my assessment proposal over to the solicitor I spoke with earlier. As I wait for the fax to connect, I begin wondering if he gets paid for speaking with me, because I won't get paid for speaking with him, unless I am contracted for this task.
6.30pm	Head to airport for late flight to Scotland to begin new assessment with family first thing tomorrow.
9.00pm	Arrive in Scotland and receive a telephone call from my office, to say that those court papers have just arrived by courier!
9.30pm	Check into hotel, check my emails, prepare for tomorrow's first meeting.

10.01pm	Go down to the restaurant to order some dinner, only to find that the restaurant closed at 10.00pm.
10.05pm	Check my emails. A colleague has emailed me to inform me that she has been asked to chair some seminars next week but cannot make it, and has therefore recommended me to her contact.
10.10pm	I telephone home and ask my partner to kiss the children for me and put the dog out!
10.15pm	With a half-eaten bag of sweets and a pitiful cup of tea, I sit back in a child-sized chair, miles from home, savouring the thought of not having to take the dog out to the park in the morning, fantasising about how I might chair next week's seminar, and trying to answer the most important question of the day…did I work smarter, not harder? There must be an easier way…

Notes on the contributor
Eddie O'Hara is a registered social worker and qualified primary teacher. Since starting his social work career over twenty years ago, Eddie has worked in a variety of children and family settings. Since 2000, Eddie has worked as a full-time independent social worker/consultant, and has developed both a growing interest and reputation in assessing/consulting on potential kinship placements. In recent years, Eddie's work has taken him throughout the UK, Ireland and California (USA).

Chapter 10

Assessment and Transferable Skills

Anne Sambidge

The common theme running through the many and varied assessments that I have carried out during the past eleven years as an independent social worker has been the complexity of the contracts. Critical decisions with life-changing implications have often been made on the basis of conclusions I have reached. The risks to service users of getting it wrong are incalculable, the responsibility immense. As a sole practitioner there is no hiding place, the buck stops right here.

The following case summary, suitably anonymised, illustrates this.

Referral

This case started in an extraordinary way with a tense telephone call from the courtroom itself. Blurting out that she was standing in front of a Judge as she spoke, a child care Team Manager asked whether I could urgently assess a paternal aunty and her male partner as carers for the aunty's three and six-year-old nieces? With the Manager acting as intermediary, the Judge outlined his condition: the aunty must separate physically and emotionally from her brother, the girls' father, for he had seriously injured one of the girls. We agreed a tight deadline for my assessment.

The assessment and some dilemmas

I familiarised myself with the current literature and research on family members as 'custodial carers' whilst awaiting the court bundle. This gave little information about the children themselves so I went to read the children's files. It became evident that a critical shortage of social work staff had resulted in a minimal service to the little girls.

I obtained the views of the foster carers about the children before getting to know them and then meeting their aunty and her partner. During one home visit the aunty received a telephone call from her brother. Afterwards she confirmed that the two were in close contact, both determined to continue their relationship. Against the wishes of all other parties, who wanted the assessment to continue, I asked for the court's opinion for I believed it was unethical to continue with my assessment once it was clear that the condition set by the Judge had been breached.

In due course the aunty and I gave evidence in court about her ongoing involvement with her brother. The Judge ordered my assessment to cease and dismissed the aunty's application. There was an unpleasant scene, which resulted in the police being called after a witness was attacked by the birth family.

In due course I submitted my invoice for the assessment. Weeks rolled past so I began the time-consuming exercise of pursuing payment, vowing that any future contract I undertook would state very specific terms, particularly that I would charge interest for late payment. At a similar time I received threatening letters from the aunty's partner. Learning that Royal Mail was obliged to disclose the location of my PO Box number if requested (before this time I was neither aware that this was the case nor that I could seek to have my address withheld), I took safety precautions as I came and went from my home where my office is based. Eventually, the letters stopped.

Transferable skills

Soon after I received payment and just when I thought it was all over, the girls' social worker asked if I could prepare them for the adoption placement that had been identified for them.

In theory it was an attractive piece of work. I had acquired extensive knowledge about the family background and I had experience of working directly with children. Even so, the work proved a huge challenge. Despite considerable efforts, I couldn't identify appropriate 'tools' to assist me when working towards adoption with a three-year-old whose developmental delay was only just becoming apparent. Not for the first time, I was forced to fall back upon my own resources to find suitable materials to help her track, in a simplistic way befitting her stage of development, her route from birth to her current foster home. This work, plus the photos in the life-story book, which I put together with and for her, provided the backdrop for introducing the 'welcome book' from her adoptive parents.

The work with the six-year-old was even more testing. Unusually given her age, this little girl appeared to have no concept of 'family'. Realising I was out of my depth, it occurred to me that the child's class teacher might have some ideas. Her response was to invite me to meet her, her classroom assistant and the Special Needs Co-ordinator to discuss exactly what was needed. We explored together how the school might help, recognising that we had only one chance to get it right.

Based on what I had told them, teaching staff devised a five-week programme. This built upon the child's existing skills in logic and was geared to the date when introductions between the girls and their adoptive family would start. The programme involved an individual session with the classroom assistant each morning to develop the child's general understanding of the concept of grouping. Afternoon sessions were designed to establish the idea of family groupings specifically through selected reading of books such as *The Three Billy Goats Gruff* and *Goldilocks and the Three Bears* combined with discussions about the stories. As school holidays intervened, my role was to continue the work through daily visits to the child at her foster home, engaging her in, for example, sorting the jumbled contents of a big bag into piles of similar items, playing Happy Families card games and sorting different types of bean bag 'babies' into their obvious 'families'. Over the five weeks this little girl's understanding of families developed dramatically - to the point that she was ready to meet the people whom she herself had identified as 'my new family'.

This case study illustrates that to be truly effective as an independent social work practitioner it is necessary to have both key skills and particular personal attributes. Independent social work is not for everyone. I have found that proven social work skills and a wealth of social work experience are absolute imperatives, along with the ability to assess the appropriateness of a referral and the confidence and the courage to decide whether or not to accept it. Critical analysis skills plus the ability to report in writing and deliver on time are crucial. During the eleven years that I have been working independently it has become progressively important to be familiar with current research and practice and to be willing to put in the time, effort and training to acquire this knowledge.

Anyone who does their job well makes it look easy; independent social work is no different. Running a small business is not always as simple as it might seem. Practising alone can be onerous and stressful, so having a peer group and a consultant/mentor to bounce ideas off are essential. As it is usually the contentious piece of work that is contracted out of an organisation, it is particularly important to be aware of, and guard against, being conveniently but wrongly used as 'the fall guy'.

It is frequently difficult to get the balance of work right for cases often come back in different guises, as the case study demonstrates. This shows, too, how freedom to use my own initiative led to a tremendously important partnership with the school, enabling professionals from different disciplines to work very effectively together in the interests of the child.

Notes on the contributor
Anne Sambidge qualified as a social worker in 1971. Initially she worked as a generic social worker then in posts enabling her to develop her interest in mental health, work with stepfamilies and in family placement. In 1994 Anne set up a small business as an Independent social work practitioner. Since then she has worked on commissions from Family Placement and Children and Families teams, fitting various part-time academic and post-qualifying courses around contracts.

Chapter 11

Emergency Duty Teams

Anita Traynor

Having come from a background in children and family area teams I am very conscious that although social workers will frequently still be completing the day's work when the office closes, the answerphone clicks on at this time giving the Emergency Duty Team's (EDT) number. So who are the professionals dealing then with the public?

I must admit that, as a day worker, I never thought too much about the work EDTs undertake, other than being thankful to be 'off duty'. I was particularly pleased, therefore, when my company was contracted to provide a short-term contract manager to such a team. One intriguing part of the role is that whilst it involves responsibility for the management of a team that works overnight, weekends and Bank Holidays, the management role is predominately carried out in the daytime.

It was essential to work a few of the shifts with the team in order to meet the team members, to understand the work systems and to see how the team members related to one another. This was a real 'eye-opener' to me, seeing a generic team covering all aspects of social work from community care, child protection and mental health assessments, to assessing homeless people, acting as appropriate adults with vulnerable witnesses and much more in between. (This runs contrary to the current daytime model where policy has shifted to specialised work in multi-disciplinary teams.) This small team of only eight permanent qualified social workers is supplemented by sessional qualified social workers, who cover gaps in the rota. In this setting where expertise is at a premium, there are no unqualified social workers, but I was interested to note that social work students value placements with the team.

Supervision is very important in such a team but the style is quite different from the daytime work as there are not the same service user targets to achieve as in direct work and fewer meetings or reviews to attend. The focus is on developing good professional practices across the very wide area of work covered by the team and team relationships. There is also emphasis upon links with other agencies such as the police, crisis mental health team and local hospitals who share the experience of working 'out of hours'.

I wondered if there would be difficulties in recruitment but I discovered that some members of this team have been in post for over twenty years, which speaks very well for their sense of job satisfaction. I understand that staff turnover and sickness rates are much lower in this sector generally, in marked contrast to my recent experiences of daytime services, where teams are affected by high staff turnover, sickness and significant use of agency staff.

I have come to appreciate that whilst EDT shifts can be very stressful and busy, dealing with crises and awaiting the next telephone call, there is certainty that once that shift is finished all the work is completed. Every telephone call taken by the EDT results in a piece of work that is followed by a report, which is faxed to the area team ready for their next working day. Once that fax has gone that is the end of the EDT's involvement - no need for long-term planning or ongoing assessments. This provides what for social workers is the relatively rare sense of 'task completion' on a regular basis.

Another unexpected bonus is that the same service user may be spoken to again and again by the team. There are 'regulars' (as in the daytime duty service) who keep the team updated on every detail of their lives. There is even one regular caller who rings in to offer their view of the best racing tips for the next day! For many of these people EDTs fill a gap in their lives. It is not usually possible for very busy daytime departments to be available to service users who feel the need for a 'chat' and to pass the time of day. The EDT, however, can manage a number of such contacts during quiet periods and as these people are regular callers, they are very accepting if told that due to incoming emergency work pressures, the conversation has to end quite quickly.

I was very uncertain about the pressures of working shifts, but colleagues who have remained in this area of work for long periods say they have become accustomed to this and find that they can fit other things around it with comparative comfort. Teams generally operate from 4.30pm to 9am the next day in the normal working week and 24-hour cover is provided for weekends and Bank Holidays. This means that seventy-five per cent of the time in the working week is covered by EDTs. Of course, there has to be an approved social worker (ASW) to cover statutory mental health work, on all shifts whether in person or 'on call', as needed. The most challenging shift is definitely from 1am to 9am each morning, when there is usually only one social worker on duty, which calls for considerable professional ability and a steady nerve.

When the telephone rings there is an air of expectancy. As the EDT is a generic team, the calls can vary from cancelling a home carer for that evening, to undertaking a mental health assessment or dealing with a child protection issue. It is a very close working environment with social workers working in the same office, often pooling ideas on cases based upon past experiences and supporting one another. It is one of the most important aspects of EDT work that social workers are experienced enough to work with little or no background information and to work solely with the presenting problem, not able to speak immediately to contacts in other agencies. Imagine dealing with a child protection case without being able to speak to someone at the school, or to the health visitor. In this respect there are many parallels with independent social work.

Mental health issues can also be very challenging. This team has support from a back-up mental health crisis team, which can deal with a number of difficult mental health service users and to whom the EDT can refer. Saturday and Sunday mornings tend to be very busy for the ASW. Sometimes service users requiring a mental health assessment have drunk a lot of alcohol the previous evening and the ASW has to be satisfied that they are well enough before they can be assessed.

Probably amongst the most concerning type of calls are those from people who clearly say they want to commit suicide. In common with other telephone helplines, on occasions EDT workers suspect that they have been the last person that a distressed caller spoke to, before killing themselves. This is not an easy thought to live with and this is where support from experienced colleagues is so important.

So where is the manager in all this? A key part of the role is to take part in the 'on-call' cover whenever the team is working. In my view this can be the most difficult part of the job of managing the team, as you can be called in the early hours of the morning, with details of extreme child abuse or some other emergency. You have to think on your feet and support your colleague, whilst only half awake. After agreeing what action is to be followed and making sure that the worker has the support they require, you put the telephone down. Trying to go to sleep again can be impossible as the case goes round and round in your head!

I know that EDT work is not for everyone but I feel privileged to have worked with such dedicated professional colleagues and I have enormous respect for the little-recognised service which delivers social work services out of office hours.

Notes on the contributor
Anita Traynor has a Psychology degree and worked at Holloway Prison's Department of Psychology for three years. Deciding that she particularly enjoyed networking with people and that work within the prison setting allowed limited opportunities for this, she went on to undertake the CQSW course at Manchester Polytechnic (now Manchester Metropolitan University) in 1990.
Since then, she has worked in various children and family teams as a practitioner and as a manager. She has gained an MSc and Diploma in Management Studies (DMS) along the way and is now an independent social worker.

Chapter 12

Social Work Consultancy

Gail C. Tucker

I fall out of bed at 5.00am. Always an early riser, I am one of those irritating people who 'does' mornings, partly because of my outdoor hobbies, but also because my work as an independent social work consultant involves travelling distances fairly frequently. The dogs get up and have breakfast and then go back to bed whilst I start the day with several cups of tea and yesterday's email. It is early Autumn and the joys of early rising are less obvious in the dark mornings, but the peace and quiet of an office without a ringing telephone is not to be underestimated. This is a good time for thinking and finalising detailed documents.

For the independent social work consultant working from home, the management of the competing demands of several corporate clients is one of the fundamental issues. If you fail to maintain the balance between their demands and the rest of your life, then the main benefits of running your own business are lost.

When I set up my social work consultancy over eleven years ago, I realised that it was vital to have a clear plan about what level of work I wanted to take on. Almost all consultants report that their work comes by personal recommendation and that there is generally more work than there is time to do it in! These days I plan to work two days a week in the office and two on the road, with one left over for what I want to do, but it does not always work out like that. However, when I feel that it is getting out of balance only I have both a clear idea about what needs to be done and the power to adjust it!

With the desk reasonably clear I can go and do the morning rounds of the livestock (population varies but always includes my horse, hens, dogs and several cats). Having returned and transformed back into the tidier and be-suited 'me', I am ready to commence my day of professional consultancy work but first I throw some dinner in the oven and set the timer - as nights draw in, it is very comforting to arrive home to the smell of something cooking!

I am out and about today, so by 9.00am I am already enroute for my destination - a care home for older people, located some hundred miles north of where I am based in Staffordshire. One of my major clients, a national legal helpline, commissions me to avert de-registration proceedings under the Care Standards Act (2000), which may be affecting their policyholders. Today's case involves a serious case of alleged abuse of a resident by a staff member. The Protection of Vulnerable Adults investigation has already commenced.

My task here today is to assess what needs to change in the home's care policies and procedures to address the issues that have already become obvious from the preliminary enquiries. This done, I shall assist the management to implement these and also liaise with both Social Services colleagues (as the lead investigating agency) and Inspectors from the Commission for Social Care Inspection, until we are all satisfied that the home represents a safe environment for service users and staff. The role involves expertise in the practice and legal requirements in this legislation but also advocacy and troubleshooting abilities, to gain the confidence of all the parties and work in a consensus model to avert use of regulatory action. The bottom line is the alleviation of risk to the service users and the staff working in the service.

Just before lunch an urgent call on my mobile is from another client, a national charity to whom I provide consultancy, who want me to be in London in two days' time, to advise their business unit heads on an urgent compliance matter that has just arisen. This means juggling of my diary but three telephone calls later it is arranged and a meeting with another London client is 'slotted-in' for the same day.

Not all independent social workers enjoy this type of pressure, with several customers with competing demands and inevitable conflicts of timetables.

The constant re-assessing of priorities is a regular feature of the type of consultancy I offer and although it can be frustrating at times, it must be remembered that this is part of what organisations are seeking from you. In buying in your expertise they are also purchasing flexibility and availability which they do not have within their resources. This comes at a premium, of course, and the important thing is to be very clear that you are the one who determines the priorities. It means that no two days are ever alike!

Driving back to the office, later in the afternoon, I listen to my voicemails via the hands-free mobile in the car. Technology has made life much easier for busy professionals but it can mean that you are always 'on-duty'. I return calls to an instructing solicitor in an expert witness case that I am preparing and to a BASW colleague, who asks me to speak at a meeting on professional conduct in social work practice. I agree, even though I am pretty busy at the moment, because I am passionate about higher ethical standards in practice and am currently studying Ethics in Social Welfare, particularly important at this time of the new Registration of the social work profession.

I consider myself very fortunate to be able to make the equivalent of one day a week, on average, available for activities where I put something back into my profession. My roles within BASW, being a Board member of the Social Care Institute for Excellence and Honorary Secretary of the Social Workers' Benevolent Trust fulfil this objective. It is one of the major satisfactions of running my own business that I am able to make these contributions and I also benefit from meeting a huge range of fascinating people along the way.

When I arrive home, it is off to the office first, despite a huge greeting from the dogs who are patiently waiting for their evening walk. More emails and today's post to check first. One or two immediate replies have to be made (email does tend to impose a tyranny of immediacy). My mentor is gently reminding me about some work I need to send her but fortunately, as I am in the office tomorrow preparing materials for a training day, I can finish this off then.

The oven 'pings' to announce that the dinner is ready and this is the opportunity for a family 'catch up' on the day. Bringing the working day to an end is a discipline that has to be acquired when you work from home. It can be hard to do, but I know that it is now time to close the office door, to mark the separation between work and home.

Just time for the evening dog walk, this time to feed my long suffering horse 'Sunshine' and to spend the twilight hour outdoors with them, the hens, the cats and our local colony of bats. The perfect antidote to a busy day...!

Notes on the contributor

Gail C. Tucker qualified as a social worker in 1975 and practised in local authorities until 1989. She subsequently worked UK-wide and has extensive experience of representing professionals in formal proceedings including tribunals and public inquiries.

Since 1994, Gail has operated her own company as an independent social work consultant and currently acts for several national organisations, advising on Care Standards Act compliance and providing expert witness in the courts.

She is currently Co-Chair of the Independents' Forum, having chaired the organisation since its inception.

Chapter 13
Expert Witness

Colin Luger

Some independent social workers and consultants find themselves working in the court domain, where their experience and expertise are valued. This chapter focuses on Family and High Court proceedings, but an independent social worker may find themselves in other legal settings, advising lawyers or contributing to Tribunals.

Opinion

When you enter the court domain as an expert witness you must recognise that your role has changed to that of adviser to the Court. You are not there to be therapeutic but usually to account for the work you have done or to provide an opinion on the work of other social work professionals. Your evidence will only be an opinion and in the interests of justice will be examined and weighed.

Recent concerns about the evidence of expert witnesses have raised a debate about their purpose and function, including the issue of when experts stray out of their area of expertise. As an expert your first duty is to the court, not to the person who pays you.

Instructions

As an expert witness you will become involved usually through an enquiry from one of the parties to the proceedings or their legal representatives. It is helpful to have your current fee scale and your Curriculum Vitae up to date and in electronic format. It is likely that they will ask for an initial estimate of the costs of the work, on only the very minimum of information about the extent of the work. Make sure that you make it clear what is an estimate and what is a firm undertaking.

Some enquirers will wish to take up references from parties in previous cases you have dealt with, so keep a current list of referees who have already given their consent to be used. You may also be asked for dates when you are available for professionals' meetings and hearings, so it is helpful to keep your diary of available dates to hand.

Always ask enquirers to keep you informed of the progress of a possible referral, otherwise you may receive a letter of instruction and a filing date you have not agreed to! A letter of instruction will come from the lead solicitor, who is the legal representative with whom you should have all contact. This will set out the issues you are to address, which have been established by the court. Read through the questions and check that they are within your area of expertise - if not, advise the lead solicitor straight away.

Check the date your report has to be filed and that you can comply; you should allow a few days for your report to reach the lead solicitor, for it to be filed at the Court by the due date, and for it to be circulated to all parties.

Always insist that before you commence work you have a letter of instruction. If you are instructed jointly, the letter of instruction will previously have been circulated to parties for agreement, which can take time as the issues might be varied or added to.

Time management

Courts have to work to strict timetables and can be frustrated by the delay in engaging an expert who is in demand. However interesting the case may sound, do remember to keep a clear sense of how much work you can sensibly do and be aware that writing the report will require considerable 'thinking time' before you even start setting finger to keyboard.

Deadlines will rush towards you but beware of compromising your professionalism in trying to work too quickly. At the same time, delay in determining cases in court must be avoided, so a balance must be achieved between reasonable efficiency and professional thoroughness.

Preparation

Your instruction will inevitably be accompanied by a bundle of court documents that you will have to read and analyse before commencing your assessment. Do not underestimate how long it will take to read the bundle. Papers need to be tabulated and each document placed in date order, to assist ease of reference later on. If you have been given an edited bundle, you may need to request further documents if they are relevant to your enquiries.

As you read, keep a brief note of the document title, its contents and any relevant points that relate to your assessment so that you can refer to your notes during interviews. Use genograms, eco-maps and critical incident pathways as you go along to help you identify who's who in the family network, the professional network, and the chronology of significant events and concerns.

Interviews and professional meetings

When arranging interviews it is advisable to confirm the appointment in writing and copy the letter to the lead solicitor. It is also helpful to provide a brief leaflet for family members about yourself, your agency and how you work, with your contact telephone number. Be aware of literacy or language issues and check whether you will need an interpreter or whether you will require consultation on any cultural issues.

It is advisable to explain the issues and questions you are working to, in case they have a different understanding. You may carry out some interviews in your own premises, but it is usually important also to conduct interviews in the subject's own environment, to gain wider understanding of their environment and of their local networks. Always over-estimate the travelling time on the first visit, so that you can arrive feeling calm and punctual. Keep a careful record of all your contacts, whether face-to-face, by telephone, letter, fax or email, as you may be questioned in court about them.

Although professionals' meetings are less formal than a court hearing, a record will be made, which will be part of the proceedings, so consider any contributions you make there very carefully as if you were on the witness stand.

Reports

Until you give evidence in court your report has to speak for you. The format is fairly standard and can be learnt. As well as identifying the legislation involved and the subject(s) of your report, you must accurately describe who you are, your qualifications, experience, your area of expertise, the questions and issues you have been asked to address, the documents you have read as part of your assessment and who you have had contact with in its preparation.

The report needs to include such detail as will enable the reader to make sense of your opinion later in the report, so decide how much will provide clarity without overwhelming the reader with unnecessary detail.

As you write, it can be helpful to focus your thinking by imagining standing in the witness box and responding to hostile questions about your report. Your opinion will be in response to the questions posed in the letter of instruction but you may be aware that it would assist the court to elaborate further than the question posed - be helpful but take care not to step outside your area of expertise.

You should conclude with your recommendation and the following sentence:

> *I declare that this report is true to the best of my knowledge, information and belief, and I understand it will be placed before the court.*

Appearing in Court

Unless you are very experienced or confident about your courtroom skills, it is advisable to attend a courtroom skills course.

Appearing in court as an expert witness will bring you into a frustrating domain of delay and hearings that inevitably do not take place at the appointed time. Many matters are dealt with by the lawyers in the corridors or consulting rooms. Remember that as a witness you are not permitted to have conversations with parties or their legal representatives about the case, unless a meeting has been convened and recorded.

Hearings vary in length according to whether they are directions or final and you will only be asked to attend as required, for which you will need to provide an advance estimate of costs of your attendance. Sometimes you will not be called at all, because matters have been settled without your needing to give evidence.

Useful guidance can be found at www.hmcourts-service.gov.uk and Wall, N (2000) *Expert Witnesses in Children Act Cases*. Bristol, Family Law.

Colin Luger is a social worker, and a family therapist and systemic practitioner. He has worked in a local authority, the NSPCC, and is currently working independently as an expert in Courts in England and Wales with serious child protection concerns. He is a member of the Independents' Forum of BASW, teaches on the University of the West of England's 'Issues in Child Protection' course and is an honorary family therapist with an NHS Trust.

Chapter 14

Ethical Practice

Gail C. Tucker

Some twenty years ago or more, there was probably a consensus that 'private' social work practice, as it was then called, could not be ethical. In the early twenty-first century, not only is independent work much more prevalent, but it is also recognised as representing very high-quality social work practice. This does set some very high expectations upon you when you decide to embark upon a career as an independent social worker or consultant.

In the initial stages, it is the practical issues of how you are going to find work and how you are going to pay the bills that tend to dominate your thinking. Elsewhere in this book these matters are addressed in some detail and cautionary advice is given about ensuring that you have put in place the building blocks of good business practice.

In the pressures of that turbulent time it is equally crucial to give the same amount of attention to making sure that you have addressed the demands of good ethical practice.

Supervision, consultation or mentoring

One of the immediate changes from working for a social work employer will be that there is now no other formal framework for accountability. This, you may well feel, is generally a good thing as it is one of the main causes of frustration in a professional career. This euphoria must be tempered with the recognition that you, as proprietor of your new social work business, are now solely responsible for the legal and ethical accountability of your practice.

It is an expectation of professional social work practice that you will put in place arrangements that are suitable for your needs, to provide yourself with high-quality professional support from a supervisor, consultant or mentor (depending upon your assessed requirements). You may need to make financial provision for this although it can often be achieved on a 'no cost' reciprocal basis with another colleague or group of colleagues.

It is wise to identify an arrangement at the earliest opportunity, in order that the terms and the nature of this working relationship of trust have been established before any difficulties arise to put it to the test. It is also advisable to have a formal contract to ensure that there is complete understanding of the nature of the relationship, rules about confidentiality and where the responsibility lies for business matters.

Registration and Post-Registration Training and Learning (PRTL)

If the basis on which your customers will retain your services as an independent social worker or consultant is derived from your social work qualification, knowledge and experience, then you should be registered with the Care Council in the country in the UK where your business is based. If you have left public sector work, you will probably already have a Registration but you need to take account of the fact that you are now fully responsible for the provision of your own PRTL.

This will involve setting aside time for assessing your professional needs and planning your training opportunities. In addition, you need to make financial provision to pay for courses and, of course, the time to complete them. This will involve you setting aside funds to cover your income for those days when you are not earning fees!

Independent social workers and consultants proudly proclaim their profession. For them, social work is not just an occupation but an intrinsic part of their identity. For this highly motivated group, of very well-qualified and experienced professionals, there is the dual responsibility of contributing to the development of the profession, as well as benefiting from it. This can constitute part of their Professional Development Plan.

Particularly in roles where independent practitioners are commissioned to carry out investigations cases involving complaints against other registered social workers, or where expert evaluation of their work is called for by the Courts and Tribunals it is considered highly likely that Registration will be regarded as essential and will become a condition of many contracts over time.

Professional Conduct and Ethics

Registration represents a benchmark of agreed standards of practice, which are well documented in the Codes of Practice for Social Care Employees and Employers. These are the same in each of the countries of the UK, fully transparent and offer a degree of security for all parties against potential professional difficulties that may arise in relation to a contract. There is an outside body to whom the individual is accountable for their professional conduct, with expectations about their continuing professional development and with formal procedures for managing complaints, should the need arise.

Ethical practice arises from the core identity of professional social workers. Members of BASW have been bound by a Code of Ethics since the early 1970s. The current version of this Code establishes a set of values along with a series of principles that underpin practice within these:

- Human dignity and worth.
- Social justice.
- Service to humanity.
- Integrity.
- Competence.

Independent social work is now separately recognised within the BASW Code of Ethics and some additional responsibilities are identified. These might be considered counter to commercial objectives in other types of business, so are not things that general business advisers such as accountants or even solicitors will appreciate. Make sure you have read and fully understood the implications for your practice.

There is an absolute necessity that you should not practise outside your area of competence, including a duty to refer or advise on other, more suitable practitioners, where this issue arises. This requires you to take a cool look at where your skills and proven track record lie and to identify any training needs that might be involved in widening the skills base of your work. If you are unable to continue to provide a service you must ensure that service users are offered alternatives.

There are also expectations that you will operate your business in a way that assesses and minimises risk to those who use your services, whether they are corporate customers or individual service users. You will need to have in place the correct procedures for managing records (including Data Protection Registration in respect of personal data). Whatever the type of service offered, practice records are essential for supervision and to provide good accountability for any complaint that may be made about that practice. The provision of liability insurance appropriate to your work is a necessity for the protection of your customers, as well as yourself.

It is your responsibility to make sure that conflicts of interest do not arise between your business as an independent social worker or consultant and either your private life, former employment or other part-time employed work that you may still carry out (including any agency contracts). There are usually very strict rules in employment contracts about such conflicts. It is now your duty to identify and manage the situation, as only you will have the full knowledge of the scope of your business. Where any risk of 'crossover' between two or more situations arises, you must address it straight away, alerting the parties to the situation and recommending how the conflict can be avoided. Sometimes this will require you to curtail a piece of work, and where this occurs it is important to set out the reasons carefully and in writing, to avoid subsequent misunderstanding.

The responsibilities of independent practice are considerable and if they seem onerous it may be that it is not the ideal environment for you. It is not the easy option, as many assume, but it does hold the potential for a very rewarding social work career move.

Notes on the contributor

Gail C. Tucker qualified as a social worker in 1975 and practised in local authorities until 1989. She subsequently worked UK-wide and has extensive experience of representing professionals in formal proceedings including tribunals and public inquiries.

Since 1994, Gail has operated her own company as an independent social work consultant and currently acts for several national organisations, advising on Care Standards Act compliance and providing expert witness in the courts.

She is currently Co-Chair of the Independents' Forum, having chaired the organisation since its inception.

Chapter 15

Conclusion

Helen Ogilvy, Anne Sambidge and Gail C. Tucker

Given the evidence of the foregoing chapters, it is clear that independent social work and consultancy is thriving and developing a confident, coherent professional identity. There is also space within this identity for individuality; indeed, it is almost a pre-requisite. The chapters indicate that the range of work that independent workers undertake is extensive and of a complex nature. Essential requirements for success include:

- A high level of social work skills and an ability to transfer these to a range of settings.
- Considerable experience and professional integrity.
- Constantly updated knowledge of one's area of expertise.
- An honest appraisal of one's limitations as well as one's skills.
- A clear understanding of professional and business responsibilities as well as clarity of ethical stance.
- Motivation and resilience, particularly on days when the going is tough.
- Good organisational skills.
- Good communication and presentation skills.
- A network of support and supervision.
- An ability to construct and maintain a work/life balance whilst being flexible about working hours, depending upon the needs of customers at any given time.

What is also clear from the experiences of contributors to this book is that if one is able to meet the above requirements, independent social work and consultancy can offer a very creative and fulfilling avenue through which to develop one's career. It offers the opportunity to develop skills and knowledge in a chosen area of expertise and to work in considerable detail with one's clients, whether individual or corporate. Indeed, much of the in-depth and therapeutic practice that used to be an integral part of the role of social workers within Local Authorities is now firmly located within the independent sector.

Many independent social workers and consultants also find it possible to work in a less defensive culture, where they are able to take a more positive view of risk and work with it more creatively. Many find it easier to work more closely within the spirit of the Codes of Practice and the BASW Code of Ethics than they did in previous employment and this brings an increased level of job satisfaction.

This does not mean that independent social workers and consultants have *carte blanche* to practise in a risky way or, indeed, any way they choose. Independent practitioners are, and always have been, bound by the same professional codes and legislative frameworks as fellow professionals. However, with the arrival of the Care Councils and registration requirements, there is arguably a more obvious framework to underpin practice and against which to judge independent practitioners.

Above all else, one thing seems clear. Independent social work and consultancy exist and have a valid place in the bright spectrum of social work services in the UK. Independent social workers and consultants are not lost to the profession - individually and collectively, they are a valuable resource for the profession and for the public.

Returning to the title of this book, is independent social work a risky business? As one might expect from a text written by social workers, the answer to this question is both yes and no. It is risky in the sense that any business carries risk - part of the skill lies in recognising, evaluating and managing the risks. It is also risky in the sense that one has to work effectively with risk, whether with individuals or with organisations - but many people find that this can be a positive aspect of their work, not a problematic one. For many, risk is something to be embraced, not feared. Perhaps the most telling calculation for many independent practitioners has been the evaluation of the risks of choosing the path to independence as opposed to the risks of remaining where they were. The reality is that for those social workers with the right skills, experience and aptitudes, the risks are manageable, but it is not right for everyone. It is not an easy option, but it is one that brings challenge, professional development opportunities and, often, a sense of achievement. Those who have contributed to this book would tell you that, for them, it was a risk worth taking.

Appendix

Some Useful Websites

Action on Elder Abuse
www.elderabuse.org.uk

Age Concern
www.ageconcern.org.uk

Alzheimer's Society
www.alzheimers.org.uk

Barnardo's
www.barnardos.org.uk

British Association for the Study and Prevention of Child Abuse and Neglect
www.baspcan.org.uk

British Association of Social Workers
www.basw.co.uk

BASW Independents' Forum
www.basw.co.uk/if

BASW Independents Online
www.search4socialworkers.com

British Institute of Learning Disability
www.bild.org.uk

Community Legal Service Direct
www.justask.org.uk

Care Councils:
  General Social Care Council (England) www.gscc.org.uk
  Care Council for Wales www.ccwales.org.uk
  Scottish Social Services Council www.sssc.uk.com
  Northern Ireland Social Care Council www.niscc.info

Care and Health
www.careandhealth.co.uk

Carers UK
www.carers.demon.co.uk

Children Webmag
www.childrenwebmag.com

Community Care magazine
www.communitycare.co.uk

Companies House
www.companieshouse.gov.uk

Courts Service
www.hmcourts-service.gov.uk

Cruse
www.crusebereavementcare.org.uk

Data Protection Registrar
www.dataprotection.gov.uk

Dementia Research Centre
www.dementia.ion.ucl.ac.uk

Department of Health
www.dh.gov.uk

Department for Education and Skills
www.dfes.gov.uk

Disabled Living Foundation
www.dlf.org.uk

Disability Rights Commission
www.drc-gb.org

Every Child Matters
www.everychildmatters.gov.uk

Federation of Small Businesses
www.fsb.org.uk

Guardian 24
www.bluechiptechnologies.com

Help the Aged
www.helptheaged.org.uk

HM Revenue and Customs (VAT)
www.hmrc.gov.uk

Information for Local Government
www.info4local.gov.uk

MENCAP
www.mencap.org.uk

Mental Health Foundation
www.mentalhealth.org.uk

Mind
www.mind.org.uk

National Children's Bureau
www.ncb.org.uk

National Society for the Prevention of Cruelty to Children
www.nspcc.org.uk

Royal Mail
www.royalmail.com

Royal National Institute for the Blind
www.rnib.org.uk

Royal National Institute for the Deaf
www.rnid.org.uk

Self-Directed Support
(people with learning disabilities achieving greater control over their lives)
www.in-control.org.uk

Social Care Institute for Excellence
www.scie.org.uk

SCOPE
www.scope.org.uk